Ammon and the Sheep

written by Tiffany Thomas
illustrated by Nikki Casassa

CFI • An imprint of Cedar Fort, Inc • Springville, Utah

HARD WORDS:
Ammon, sheep, afraid, learn

PARENT TIP: If the child feels overwhelmed, cover the following words so they only see one word. Do not cover the pictures.

This is Ammon.
He is a son
of King Mosiah.

These are Lamanites.
They do not know God.

Ammon wants to teach the Lamanites.

Ammon meets King Lamoni.

King Lamoni tells Ammon
to take care of his sheep.

Bad men take the sheep.
God helps Ammon save the sheep.

Ammon cuts off
the arms of
the bad people who
tried to hurt him.

King Lamoni is afraid of Ammon.

Ammon says he is from God.

King Lamoni wants to
learn about God.

Ammon is happy.

The end.

ISBN 13: 978-1-4621-4337-5

Published by CFI, an imprint of Cedar Fort, Inc. • 2373 W. 700 S., Suite 100, Springville, UT 84663
Distributed by Cedar Fort, Inc., www.cedarfort.com

Cover design and interior layout design by Shawnda T. Craig
Cover design © 2022 Cedar Fort, Inc.
Printed in China • Printed on acid-free paper
10 9 8 7 6 5 4 3 2 1